THE BUT SNATCHER

Written by Beverley and Ian Reynolds
Illustrated by Ian Reynolds

CollinsEducational
An Imprint of HarperCollinsPublishers

One evening at the cinema, as the audience sat watching the latest creepy film, a long thin bony hand crept amongst them

from trouser leg

to cardigan,

from blouse

to blazer,

carefully choosing what it wanted.

No-one noticed a hooded figure in the darkness.

No-one saw the glint of steel as a blade briefly caught the film's rays of light.

No-one heard the *snip snip* of sharpened scissors followed by a muffled chuckle. They were all watching the film.

If they had looked down beneath the rows of seats, they might have seen a scraggy, thin man crawling over the fizzy pop cans and sticky sweets, searching for buttons cut from the audience's clothing.

And if they had been looking at the exit just before the end of the film, they might have seen his shadow for an instant, before the door closed silently behind him. *But nobody did see him.*

As the lights went up and the audience started to leave their seats...

DISASTER STRUCK!

IT'S GONE COLD IN HERE.

I MUST GO ON THAT DIET I PROMISED MYSELF.

DO UP YOUR COAT ARTHUR. YOU WILL CATCH A COLD!

I DON'T SEEM TO BE ABLE TO FIND MY BUTTONS, DEAR (GULP!).

In a dark, dirty building down a rubbish-filled alley, stood an old warehouse, long since forgotten. Inside, by the light of a single light bulb, huddled Jackson Spindley, the same thin, bony man from the cinema that night. He was counting buttons on a huge table top.

Two hours later...

It had been a successful night at the cinema.

Spindley hadn't cared much for the film but he had collected **more** buttons than he had **dared** to imagine.

He was very pleased with his Raspberry Bip-Bop collection, but he still had a lot of counting and checking and box-filing to do before morning.

Now, who is Jackson Spindley?
Let's take a closer look...

WHO IS JACKSON SPINDLEY?

ARMY SURPLUS BALACLAVA (THINKS NO-ONE CAN SEE HIM WHEN WEARING IT)

THINNING HAIR (MOST HAD BEEN PULLED OUT IN ANGER WHEN HE WENT WRONG WITH HIS BUTTON COUNTING)

GLASSES TO SEE HIS BUTTONS WITH

HOOKED NOSE CAUSED BY BEING CAUGHT IN A ZIP AS A CHILD - HAS HATED ZIPS EVER SINCE

WHO? NEVER HEARD OF HIM!

If you see Jackson Spindley he looks
quite ordinary. You wouldn't
notice him in a crowd. He wears
ordinary clothes, speaks in
an ordinary voice, walks
in an ordinary way,
but he is in fact

extraordinary...
because underneath it all,
Jackson Spindley

L O V E S   B U T T O N S.

He is button mad.

He knows every colour, size, shape and date of every
button ever made, and his dream is to be the owner
of the largest complete button collection in the
world. He has every button you could imagine:
buttons as big as your dinner plate and bigger.
Buttons as small as currants and smaller.

He could show you plastic strawberry buttons,

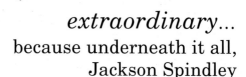

glass racing car buttons

and even woollen teddy bear buttons
(but he wouldn't!)

Here is part of his collection:

U.S. President Panic Button fitted with a homing device in case of kidnap.

Button found at Scene of Crime — helped to identify gang of smelly cheese rustlers when it appeared in a slice of Gorgonzola at a Supermarket.

Rare 1956 Jubilee Button celebrating 25 years rule by King Trot of Trotania.

• ← Smallest button in the world. Impossible to sew on.

Double-Sided Bone Button grabbed from 'Cruncher' the Terrier when wearing his new dog Jacket.

Key-Shaped costume button from actress Anita Darling, worn in a Scene on her latest T.V. Soap "Far and Beyond".

Pop Star Gary Gribson's Guitar Greats Button lost on stage in Concert in 1963.

Triple Triangle Treater taken from a maths Professor in Shapely.

Weather Button from well-known Weather man 'Gale force' Phil.

Fossil of ancient button found in Libyan desert by Dr. Oldthing on a recent dig.

And this is why, with

MILLIONS and

MILLIONS

of buttons, Spindley needs a warehouse to keep them all in and to keep prying eyes out.

BUT Spindley's collection is not complete. There is still one particular set of buttons that he desperately wants.

Over many years he has searched for the set of

PEARLY PEARLIES WITH THE PURPLE PATTERNS

but has never found them. Now they are the only buttons missing from his collection and he uses *every second* of *every day* to look for them.

What's so special about these buttons?

Spindley has made a special investigation report on the search for the **Pearly Pearlies with the Purple Patterns**.

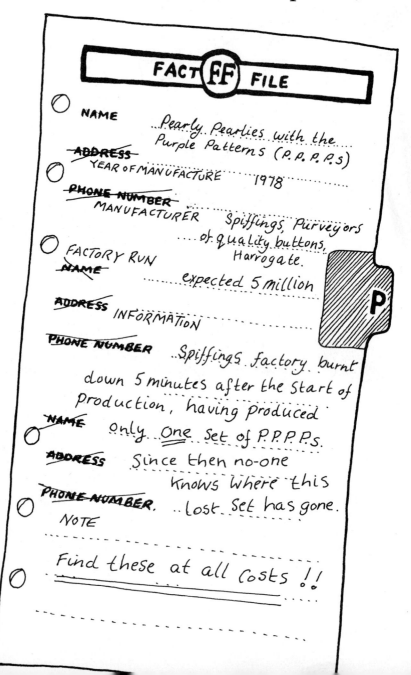

FACT (FF) FILE

○ **NAME** ...Pearly. Pearlies. with. the... Purple Patterns (P. P. P. P.s)

~~ADDRESS~~ YEAR OF MANUFACTURE ······ 1978 ·······

~~PHONE NUMBER~~ MANUFACTURER ··· Spiffings, Purveyors .... of quality buttons, Harrogate.

○ FACTORY RUN ~~NAME~~ ......expected 5 million

~~ADDRESS~~ INFORMATION ······· · · · · · · ·

~~PHONE NUMBER~~ ..Spiffings factory. burnt down 5 minutes after the start of production, having produced

○ ~~NAME~~ only. one set of P. P. P. P.s.

~~ADDRESS~~ Since then no-one knows where this

○ ~~PHONE NUMBER~~. ..lost. set has gone. NOTE ·· · · · · · · · · · · · · · · ·

○ Find these at all costs !!

P

So far, he has looked everywhere he can
think of without success.

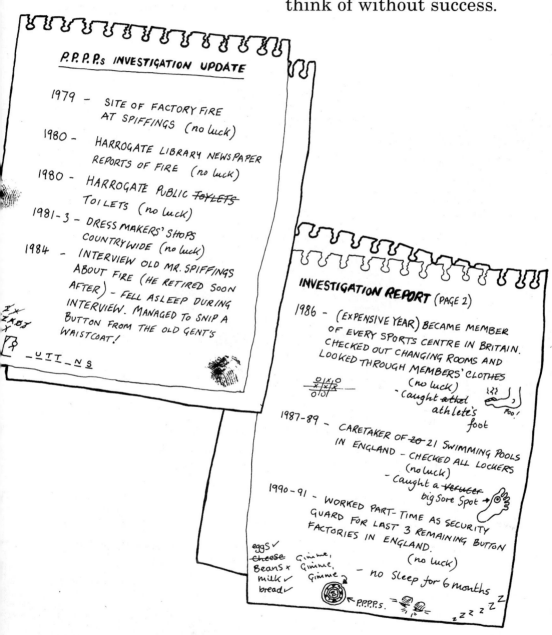

P.P.P.Ps INVESTIGATION UPDATE

1979 — SITE OF FACTORY FIRE
AT SPIFFINGS (no luck)

1980 — HARROGATE LIBRARY NEWSPAPER
REPORTS OF FIRE (no luck)

1980 — HARROGATE PUBLIC TOYLETS
TOILETS (no luck)

1981-3 — DRESS MAKERS' SHOPS
COUNTRYWIDE (no luck)

1984 — INTERVIEW OLD MR. SPIFFINGS
ABOUT FIRE (HE RETIRED SOON
AFTER) — FELL ASLEEP DURING
INTERVIEW. MANAGED TO SNIP A
BUTTON FROM THE OLD GENT'S
WAISTCOAT!

_ U T T _ N S

INVESTIGATION REPORT (PAGE 2)

1986 — (EXPENSIVE YEAR) BECAME MEMBER
OF EVERY SPORTS CENTRE IN BRITAIN.
CHECKED OUT CHANGING ROOMS AND
LOOKED THROUGH MEMBERS' CLOTHES
(no luck)
— caught athel
athlete's
foot

1987-89 — CARETAKER OF 20 21 SWIMMING POOLS
IN ENGLAND — CHECKED ALL LOCKERS
(no luck)
— caught a verucer
big sore spot

1990-91 — WORKED PART-TIME AS SECURITY
GUARD FOR LAST 3 REMAINING BUTTON
FACTORIES IN ENGLAND.
(no luck)
— no sleep for 6 months

eggs ✓
cheese
Beans ✗   Gimme,
milk ✓   Gimme,
bread ✓   Gimme

← P.P.P.P.s.

One Tuesday, Spindley decided to go button watching at Blunket Station...

YES... THERE'S A PEACHY POGGLE POPPER...

AND A TRIPLE TURNOVER...

THE USUAL STUFF I'M AFRAID.

WILL MY SEARCH NEVER END?

14

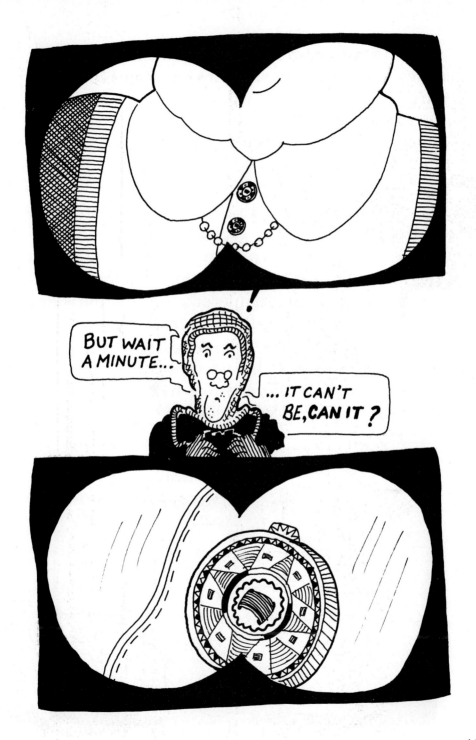

There in the crowd were the Purple shimmering Pearlies – the complete set looking breathlessly beautiful and even more wonderful than he had dared to imagine.

WOW!!!

A rather large person with a drooping moustache hid them from view for a few seconds and then their dazzling wonder shone through again. Now they were on the move and headed for platform 3, being hidden by shopping bags, bad-tempered children and a group of loud men with beer bellies. Frantically, Spindley followed the P.P.P.P.s as well as he could, almost forgetting to breathe in his excitement to own the treasures. **"I MUST have those buttons at all costs!"** said Spindley with glee.

Who is the owner of the Pearly Pearlies with the Purple Patterns?

Name: Vera Fondant
Occupation: Retired Tea Lady

INTERESTING FACTS:
Or how Miss Fondant came to own the one and only set of Pearly Pearlies with the Purple Patterns (or P.P.P.P.s)

Miss Fondant used to run a mobile sandwich bar just outside Spiffings Button Factory. She was well known for making a mean cup of tea and a custard slice.

One Wednesday afternoon in 1978, just after the first set of Pearly Pearlies with the Purple Patterns rolled off the production line, a terrible fire broke out at the factory (faulty machinery was blamed).

Bravely the fire fighters fought to put out the fire, while a daring Miss Fondant provided tea and custard slices for the exhausted crew. Finally the fire was put out and happily no-one was hurt, but the factory was in ruins.

Yoo Hoo! TEA'S UP DEARS!

OOH! THANKS.

The Fire Chief, Cuthbert Combustion, as a mark of thanks, gave Miss Fondant *something* he had found in the wreckage that had survived.

That *something* turned out to be the one and only packet of **PEARLY PEARLIES WITH THE PURPLE PATTERNS** worn proudly by Miss Fondant from that day to this.

Little did Miss Fondant know that while she was making her way home from her weekly shop at Micks & Spending's, a thin, hooded man lurking behind the Spud-U-Want stand across the station was watching her every move.

In his excitement, Spindley forgot that he was at the station where lots of people could see what he was doing. Without thinking, he rushed at Miss Fondant and accidently tore her blouse to get **HIS** buttons.

Suddenly...

With her shopping threatening to fall from her bag, Miss Fondant screamed, "You wicked man! Help me someone, he's trying to steal my fish fingers!"

"Ooh, that hurt," wailed Spindley, as Miss Fondant landed an almost deadly blow to his nose with a packet of Micks & Spending's frozen minced beef in onion gravy.

19

As if this wasn't bad enough, Miss Fondant's dog, Tiffin, also joined in the fight. He growled half-heartedly before lifting his leg and

sprinkling

PONG ???

WHIFF

DIS IS GOING TO BE BORE DIFFICUL THAN I THOR...

Spindley's shoes.

With great difficulty, Spindley finally managed to escape the savage blows from the contents of Miss Fondant's shopping bag. He dashed around the corner and hid inside a dustbin behind the Spud-U-Want stand. While he waited for the sounds of an angry Miss Fondant to calm down, he carefully picked at the remains of the fish finger Miss Fondant had jammed up his nose.

Some time later, Spindley spotted Miss Fondant and Tiffin being helped onto a train by a concerned guard.

THERE NOW MISSUS, DO YOU THINK YOU'LL BE ALL RIGHT?

RAIL STAFF

"Quite all right thank you, young man," she said as she settled into her seat. "That nasty old man ripped my blouse. I think it's ruined, but at least I won't be seeing him again!"

Spindley decided to follow and

BLUNKET STATION

MISS FONDANT'S HOUSE

think of another plan to get the buttons from her.

Soon the train stopped. Miss Fondant and Tiffin got off with a crowd of other people, while Spindley secretly followed at a distance until Miss Fondant arrived home.

HOW CAN I GET THOSE BUTTONS?
SO FAR ALL I'VE MANAGED TO
DO IS RIP HER BLOUSE.
HANG ON A SEC, THAT GIVES
ME AN IDEA...

A few days later...

"Excuse me madam," said Spindley under a cub scout hat that was several sizes too small, "I'm collecting old clothes for the Save the Sink Plunger Charity."

"I'll see what I have," said Miss Fondant, as she stepped back inside her house to have a look. Tiffin the dog sniffed Spindley's shoe. He was sure he had smelt it somewhere before.

Soon Spindley staggered away with a huge bin bag full of clothes. He was sure Miss Fondant must have thrown out her ripped blouse with the Pearly Pearlies with the Purple Patterns on it. He looked for the nearest place to empty the bag. Eagerly he vanished behind the bushes in the next door neighbour's garden.

But what did he find?

23

ZAPPO YOU KNOW IT MAKES SENSE

IT'S GOOD

ZAP!

ZAPPO 0%

WORKS AT 40°C

PPO

← WHITE SCIENTIST'S COAT

NORMAL WHITE BUTTONS →

MEGA BOX

GOOD MORNING, MADAM. WE WASHED THIS BLOUSE IN NEW IMPROVED **ZAPPO**.

The very next day, Spindley knocked again on Miss Fondant's door. He was once more in disguise, but this time he was holding a briefcase and a brand new blouse. The blouse looked just like the one Miss Fondant had before it was torn.

"Would you swap your old (and very similar blouse) for this new, snowy white one?"

"There's nothing wrong with the way I wash my clothes, thank you," said Miss Fondant. "You can keep your silly blouse. What cheek!" And with that she slammed her front door, opened her letter box and shouted after Spindley:

LETTERS

IF THE SMELL OF YOUR SHOES IS ANYTHING TO GO BY, I THINK **YOU** SHOULD BE USING ZAPPO **NOT ME!**

"I must have those buttons," thought Spindley.
"I've just got to have them.
I *long* to count them,
I *drool* over stacking them,
I *dream* of labelling and
box-filing them.
Oh yes, one day they WILL be mine!"

One week later Jackson
Spindley was no nearer to owning
the P.P.P.P.s. He was still hanging
around outside Miss Fondant's
house, with just a pocketful of
buttons to comfort him. As he stood
planning his next disguise (in fact only
his diving suit was unused), someone
suddenly ran out of Miss Fondant's
front door, straight into him.
It was a burglar with a huge
swag bag brimming over
with Miss Fondant's
belongings. The lady
herself was hot on his heels
swinging an umbrella,
shouting and trying to poke
him in his bottom.

So, who was this pesky nuisance?

25

WASHING-UP GLOVES AND CLEANING CLOTH

585714 SHIFTLEY

MEMBERS CARD
BILLY BODGITT'2 GANG
SECRET
Steal Yerstuff Stanley

Name: Stanley Shiftley
(Known as Steal Yerstuff Stan)

Occupation: Well-known local thief and house burglar. Works mainly on his own, but has been known to knock about with Billy Bodgitt's gang of crafty criminals. Not particularly bright, but always leaves burgled property **clean** and **tidy**. He has been known to dust and hoover at the scene of crime, as he takes his profession seriously and would not like to leave any prints for police to trace him. However, he can't resist rearranging furniture and flowers, fluffing up cushions and spraying air freshener.

WHO YA GUNNA CALL ...DUSTBUSTERS

BBRRR

Steal Yerstuff Stan ran straight into Spindley. In his haste to get away from Miss Fondant, he used his secret weapon – a belly-bounce – to push Spindley out of his way.

BUT WHAT A MISTAKE. Because as Spindley fell to the ground, he pulled his hands out of his pockets to save himself and then...

a sudden *pinging, bouncing, skittling, rolling* noise could be heard along the pavement – Spindley's buttons, once in his hands, had scattered everywhere, including under Stan's feet.

Rushing to get away,
Stanley dropped his bag
of swag, full of Miss
Fondant's possessions, and
hobbled as fast as he could
into the distance. "I'm not
hanging around 'ere," he
was heard to say. "I'm getting
too old for this caper. Floored by a
handful of buttons – what would me mates
say? Still I did manage to steal a nifty new Mister
Slippy floor polish!"

At that moment Miss Fondant rushed
up to thank Spindley, but before she
could congratulate him, she
noticed a gleaming,
glistening shape
on the pavement.

OH MY! ISN'T
THAT A RARE
1956 INKY-
PINKY BUTTON?
THE ONLY ONE
WITH THREE HOLES?

HOW DO
YOU KNOW
THAT?

...AND THIS IS A RED-EYED SQUINTY FROM DUNTHORP!

COR!

I'VE GOT TWO IN MY COLLECTION, BUT NOT IN SUCH GOOD CONDITION AS THIS ONE!

Miss Fondant, as it turned out, was indeed what Spindley thought could never be possible. *She was a busy button collector with a collection that nearly matched his own!* "But I thought I was the only button collector in the world," said Spindley. "I never thought anyone else would share my interest."

While Miss Fondant helped Spindley pick up the scattered buttons, she said nervously, "Quick, get the buttons into the house on the double. We don't want anyone else to see them!"

"I agree madam... they'll only want them for themselves."

Miss Fondant led Spindley by
his bony hand into her hallway
and into a dusty cupboard
under the stairs. There,
behind a false coat rack

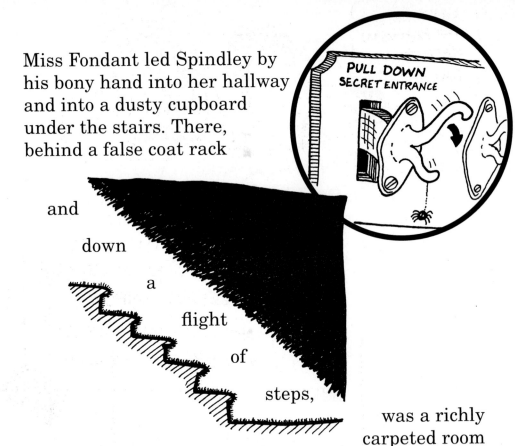

PULL DOWN
SECRET ENTRANCE

and

down

a

flight

of

steps,

was a richly
carpeted room
full of brightly coloured trays. In wonder, Spindley
pulled out tray after tray. In each one lay a
crimson velvet cushion, displaying a
precious and remarkable
collection of buttons.

SUPER CHUDD
SECURITY LOCK

Hours later, and Spindley
had seen only a fraction of Miss
Fondant's buttons. Now he
excitedly began to tell her about
his own button hoards.

Miss Fondant blushed at Spindley's compliment for her most prized possessions, but said firmly, "Mr Spindley, I have an idea. Perhaps we should join our collections together. Separately they are a huge hoard but together they would make the finest collection of buttons in the whole world! What do you say?"

Spindley's heart started to beat faster at the thought of such a dream coming true. What a brilliant future they could share together with their buttons!